higher-level thinking
QuestionS
Language Arts

questions by

Christa Chapman
Laurie Kagan
Kimberly Vincent
Arthur Lopez

created and designed by
Miguel Kagan

illustrated by
Celso Rodriguez

D1381914

Kagan

Kagan Publishing

981 Calle Amanecer

San Clemente, CA 92673

(949) 545-6300

1 (800) 933-2667

www.KaganOnline.com

ISBN: 978-1-879097-53-7

Table of Contents

> **I had six
> honest serving men
> They taught me all I knew:
> Their names were Where
> and What and When
> and Why and How and
> Who.**
>
> — Rudyard Kipling

Introduction

In your hands you hold a powerful book. It is a member of a series of transformative blackline activity books. Between the covers, you will find questions, questions, and more questions! But these are no ordinary questions. These are the important kind—higher-level thinking questions—the kind that stretch your students' minds; the kind that release your students' natural curiosity about the world; the kind that rack your students' brains; the kind that instill in your students a sense of wonderment about your curriculum.

But we are getting a bit ahead of ourselves. Let's start from the beginning. Since this is a book of questions, it seems only appropriate for this introduction to pose a few questions—about the book and its underlying educational philosophy. So Mr. Kipling's Six Honest Serving Men, if you will, please lead the way:

What?
What are higher-level thinking questions?

This is a loaded question (as should be all good questions). Using our analytic thinking skills, let's break this question down into two smaller questions: 1) What is higher-level thinking? and 2) What are questions? When we understand the types of thinking skills and the types of questions, we can combine the best of both worlds, crafting beautiful questions to generate the range of higher-level thinking in our students!

Types of Thinking

There are many different types of thinking. Some types of thinking include:

- applying
- associating
- comparing
- contrasting
- defining
- elaborating
- empathizing
- experimenting
- generalizing
- investigating
- making analogies
- planning
- prioritizing
- recalling
- reflecting
- reversing
- sequencing
- summarizing
- synthesizing
- assessing
- augmenting
- connecting
- decision-making
- drawing conclusions
- eliminating
- evaluating
- explaining
- inferring consequences
- inventing
- memorizing
- predicting
- problem-solving
- reducing
- relating
- role-taking
- substituting
- symbolizing
- understanding
- thinking about thinking (metacognition)

This is quite a formidable list. It's nowhere near complete. Thinking is a big, multifaceted phenomenon. Perhaps the most widely recognized system for classifying thinking and classroom questions is Benjamin Bloom's Taxonomy of Thinking Skills. Bloom's Taxonomy classifies thinking skills into six hierarchical levels. It begins with the lower levels of thinking skills and moves up to higher-level thinking skills: 1) Knowledge, 2) Comprehension, 3) Application, 4) Analysis, 5) Synthesis, 6) Evaluation. See Bloom's Taxonomy on the following page.

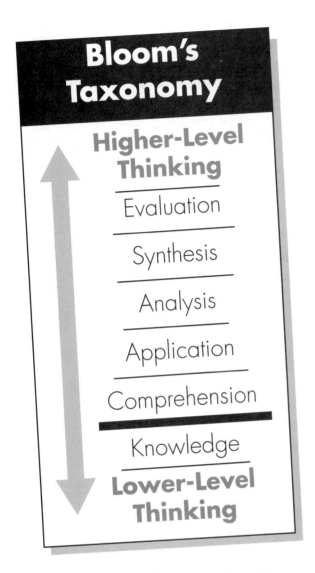

Bloom's Taxonomy

Higher-Level Thinking

Evaluation

Synthesis

Analysis

Application

Comprehension

Knowledge

Lower-Level Thinking

In education, the term "higher-level thinking" often refers to the higher levels of Mr. Bloom's taxonomy. But Bloom's Taxonomy is but one way of organizing and conceptualizing the various types of thinking skills.

There are many ways we can cut the thinking skills pie. We can alternatively view the many different types of thinking skills as, well…many different skills. Some thinking skills may be hierarchical. Some may be interrelated. And some may be relatively independent.

In this book, we take a pragmatic, functional approach. Each type of thinking skill serves a different function. So called "lower-level" thinking skills are very useful for certain purposes. Memorizing and understanding information

are invaluable skills that our students will use throughout their lives. But so too are many of the "higher-level" thinking skills on our list. The more facets of students' thinking skills we develop, the better we prepare them for lifelong success.

Because so much classroom learning heretofore has focused on the "lower rungs" of the thinking skills ladder—knowledge and comprehension, or memorization and understanding—in this series of books we have chosen to focus on questions to generate "higher-level" thinking. This book is an attempt to correct the imbalance in the types of thinking skills developed by classroom questions.

Types of Questions

As we ask questions of our students, we further promote cognitive development when we use Fat questions, Low-Consensus questions, and True questions.

Fat Questions
vs. Skinny Questions

Skinny questions are questions that require a skinny answer. For example, after reading a poem, we can ask: "Did you like the poem?" Even though this question could be categorized as an Evaluation question—Bloom's highest level of thinking— it can be answered with one monosyllabic word: "Yes" or "No." How much thinking are we actually generating in our students?

We can reframe this question to make it a fat question: "What things did you like about the poem? What things did you dislike?" Notice no short answer will do. Answering this fattened-up question requires more elaboration. These fat questions presuppose not that there is only one thing but things plural that the student liked and things that she did not like. Making things plural is one way to make skinny questions fat. Students stretch their minds to come up with multiple ideas or solutions. Other easy ways to make questions fat is to add "Why or why not?" or "Explain" or "Describe" or "Defend your position" to the end of a question. These additions promote elaboration beyond a skinny answer. Because language and thought are intimately intertwined, questions that require elaborate responses stretch students' thinking: They grapple to articulate their thoughts.

The type of questions we ask impact not just the type of thinking we develop in our students, but also the depth of thought. Fat questions elicit fat responses. Fat responses develop both depth of thinking and range of thinking skills. The questions in this book are designed to elicit fat responses—deep and varied thinking.

High-Consensus Questions vs. Low-Consensus Questions

A high-consensus question is one to which most people would give the same response, usually a right or wrong answer. After learning about sound, we can ask our students: "What is the name of a room specially designed to improve acoustics for the audience?" This is a high-consensus question. The answer (auditorium) is either correct or incorrect.

Compare the previous question with a low-consensus question: "If you were going to build an auditorium, what special design features would you take into consideration?" Notice, to the low-consensus question there is no right or wrong answer. Each person formulates his or her unique response. To answer, students must apply what they learned, use their ingenuity and creativity.

High-consensus questions promote convergent thinking. With high-consensus questions we strive to direct students *what to think*. Low-consensus questions promote divergent thinking, both critical and creative. With low-consensus

> **Education is not the filling of a pail, but the lighting of a fire.**
> — William Butler Yeats

questions we strive to develop students' *ability to think*. The questions in this book are low-consensus questions designed to promote independent, critical and creative thought.

True Questions vs. Review Questions

We all know what review questions are. They're the ones in the back of every chapter and unit. Review questions ask students to regurgitate previously stated or learned information. For example, after learning about the rain forest we may ask: "What percent of the world's oxygen does the rain forest produce?" Students can go back a few pages in their books or into their memory banks and pull out the answer. This is great if we are working on memorization skills, but does little to develop "higher-order" thinking skills.

True questions, on the other hand, are meaningful questions—questions to which we do not know the answer. For example: "What might happen if all the world's rain forests were cut down?" This is a hypothetical; we don't know the answer but considering the question forces us to think. We infer some logical consequences based on what we know. The goal of true questions is not a correct answer, but the thinking journey students take to create a meaningful response. True questions are more representative of real life. Seldom is there a black and white answer. In life, we struggle with ambiguity, confounding variables, and uncertain outcomes. There are millions of shades of gray. True questions prepare students to deal with life's uncertainties.

When we ask a review question, we know the answer and are checking to see if the student does also. When we ask a true question, it is truly a question. We don't necessarily know the answer and neither does the student. True

Types of Questions

Skinny	→	**Fat**
• Short Answer		• Elaborated Answer
• Shallow Thinking		• Deep Thinking

High-Consensus	→	**Low-Consensus**
• Right or Wrong Answer		• No Single Correct Answer
• Develops Convergent Thinking		• Develops Divergent Thinking
• "What" to Think		• "How" to Think

Review	→	**True**
• Asker Knows Answer		• Asker Doesn't Know Answer
• Checking for Correctness		• Invitation to Think

questions are often an invitation to think, ponder, speculate, and engage in a questioning process.

We can use true questions in the classroom to make our curriculum more personally meaningful, to promote investigation, and awaken students' sense of awe and wonderment in what we teach. Many questions you will find in this book are true questions designed to make the content provocative, intriguing, and personally relevant.

The box above summarizes the different types of questions. The questions you will find in this book are a move away from skinny, high-consensus, review questions toward fat, low-consensus true questions. As we ask these types of questions in our class, we transform even mundane content into a springboard for higher-level thinking. As we integrate these question gems into our daily lessons, we create powerful learning experiences. *We do not fill our students' pails with knowledge; we kindle their fires to become lifetime thinkers.*

 **Why?**
Why should I use higher-level thinking questions in my classroom?

As we enter the new millennium, major shifts in our economic structure are changing the ways we work and live. The direction is increasingly toward an information-based, high-tech economy. The sum of our technological information is exploding. We could give you a figure how rapidly information is doubling, but by the time you read this, the number would be outdated! No kidding.

But this is no surprise. This is our daily reality. We see it around us everyday and on the news: cloning, gene manipulation, e-mail, the Internet, Mars rovers, electric cars, hybrids, laser surgery, CD-ROMs, DVDs. All around us we see the wheels of progress turning: New discoveries, new technologies, a new societal knowledge and information base. New jobs are being created today in fields that simply didn't exist yesterday.

How do we best prepare our students for this uncertain future—a future in which the only constant will be change? As we are propelled into a world of ever-increasing change, what is the relative value of teaching students facts versus thinking skills? This point becomes even more salient when we realize that students cannot master everything, and many facts will soon become obsolete. Facts become outdated or irrelevant. Thinking skills are for a lifetime. Increasingly, how we define educational success will be away from the quantity of information mastered. Instead, we will define success as our students' ability to generate questions, apply, synthesize, predict, evaluate, compare, categorize.

If we as a professionals are to proactively respond to these societal shifts, thinking skills will become central to our curriculum. Whether we teach thinking skills directly, or we integrate them into our curriculum, the power to think is the greatest gift we can give our students!

We believe the questions you will find in this book are a step in the direction of preparing students for lifelong success. The goal is to develop independent thinkers who are critical and creative, regardless of the content. We hope the books in this series are more than sets of questions. We provide them as a model approach to questioning in the classroom.

On pages 8 and 9, you will find Questions to Engage Students' Thinking Skills. These pages contain numerous types of thinking and questions designed to engage each thinking skill. As you make your own questions for your students with your own content, use these question starters to help you frame your questions to stimulate

> ## Virtually the only predictable trend is continuing change.
> — Dr. Linda Tsantis,
> Creating the Future

various facets of your students' thinking skills. Also let your students use these question starters to generate their own higher-level thinking questions about the curriculum.

Who?
Who is this book for?

This book is for you and your students, but mostly for your students. It is designed to help make your job easier. Inside you will find hundreds of ready-to-use reproducible questions. Sometimes in the press for time we opt for what is easy over what is best. These books attempt to make easy what is best. In this treasure chest, you will find hours and hours of timesaving ready-made questions and activities.

Place Higher-Level Thinking In Your Students' Hands

As previously mentioned, this book is even more for your students than for you. As teachers, we ask a tremendous number of questions. Primary teachers ask 3.5 to 6.5 questions per minute! Elementary teachers average 348 questions a day. How many questions would you predict our students ask? Researchers asked this question. What they found was shocking: Typical students ask approximately one question per month.* One question per month!

Although this study may not be representative of your classroom, it does suggest that in general, as teachers we are missing out on a very powerful force—student-generated questions. The capacity to answer higher-level thinking questions is

---

* Myra & David Sadker, "Questioning Skills" in *Classroom Teaching Skills*, 2nd ed. Lexington, MA: D.C. Heath & Co., 1982.

Questions to Engage Students' Thinking Skills

Analyzing
- How could you break down…?
- What components…?
- What qualities/characteristics…?

Applying
- How is _____ an example of…?
- What practical applications…?
- What examples…?
- How could you use…?
- How does this apply to…?
- In your life, how would you apply…?

Assessing
- By what criteria would you assess…?
- What grade would you give…?
- How could you improve…?

Augmenting/Elaborating
- What ideas might you add to…?
- What more can you say about…?

Categorizing/Classifying/Organizing
- How might you classify…?
- If you were going to categorize…?

Comparing/Contrasting
- How would you compare…?
- What similarities…?
- What are the differences between…?
- How is _____ different…?

Connecting/Associating
- What do you already know about…?
- What connections can you make between…?
- What things do you think of when you think of…?

Decision-Making
- How would you decide…?
- If you had to choose between…?

Defining
- How would you define…?
- In your own words, what is…?

Describing/Summarizing
- How could you describe/summarize…?
- If you were a reporter, how would you describe…?

Determining Cause/Effect
- What is the cause of…?
- How does _____ effect _____?
- What impact might…?

Drawing Conclusions/ Inferring Consequences
- What conclusions can you draw from…?
- What would happen if…?
- What would have happened if…?
- If you changed _____, what might happen?

Eliminating
- What part of _____ might you eliminate?
- How could you get rid of…?

Evaluating
- What is your opinion about…?
- Do you prefer…?
- Would you rather…?
- What is your favorite…?
- Do you agree or disagree…?
- What are the positive and negative aspects of…?
- What are the advantages and disadvantages…?
- If you were a judge…?
- On a scale of 1 to 10, how would you rate…?
- What is the most important…?
- Is it better or worse…?

Explaining
- How can you explain…?
- What factors might explain…?

Higher-Level Thinking Questions for Language Arts
Kagan • 1 (800) 933-2667 • www.KaganOnline.com

Experimenting
- How could you test…?
- What experiment could you do to…?

Generalizing
- What general rule can…?
- What principle could you apply…?
- What can you say about all…?

Interpreting
- Why is _____ important?
- What is the significance of…?
- What role…?
- What is the moral of…?

Inventing
- What could you invent to…?
- What machine could…?

Investigating
- How could you find out more about…?
- If you wanted to know about…?

Making Analogies
- How is _____ like _____?
- What analogy can you invent for…?

Observing
- What observations did you make about…?
- What changes…?

Patterning
- What patterns can you find…?
- How would you describe the organization of…?

Planning
- What preparations would you…?

Predicting/Hypothesizing
- What would you predict…?
- What is your theory about…?
- If you were going to guess…?

Prioritizing
- What is more important…?
- How might you prioritize…?

Problem-Solving
- How would you approach the problem?
- What are some possible solutions to…?

Reducing/Simplifying
- In a word, how would you describe…?
- How can you simplify…?

Reflecting/Metacognition
- What would you think if…?
- How can you describe what you were thinking when…?

Relating
- How is _____ related to _____?
- What is the relationship between…?
- How does _____ depend on _____?

Reversing/Inversing
- What is the opposite of…?

Role-Taking/Empathizing
- If you were (someone/something else)…?
- How would you feel if…?

Sequencing
- How could you sequence…?
- What steps are involved in…?

Substituting
- What could have been used instead of…?
- What else could you use for…?
- What might you substitute for…?
- What is another way…?

Symbolizing
- How could you draw…?
- What symbol best represents…?

Synthesizing
- How could you combine…?
- What could you put together…?

a wonderful skill we can give our students, as is the skill to solve problems. Arguably more important skills are the ability to find problems to solve and formulate questions to answer. If we look at the great thinkers of the world—the Einsteins, the Edisons, the Freuds—their thinking is marked by a yearning to solve tremendous questions and problems. It is this questioning process that distinguishes those who illuminate and create our world from those who merely accept it.

Make Learning an Interactive Process

Higher-level thinking is not just something that occurs between students' ears! Students benefit from an interactive process. This basic premise underlies the majority of activities you will find in this book.

As students discuss questions and listen to others, they are confronted with differing perspectives and are pushed to articulate their own thinking well beyond the level they could attain on their own. Students too have an enormous capacity to mediate each other's learning. When we heterogeneously group students to work together, we create an environment to move students through their zone of proximal development. We also provide opportunities for tutoring and leadership. Verbal interaction with peers in cooperative groups adds a dimension to questions not available with whole-class questions and answers.

> **Asking a good question requires students to think harder than giving a good answer.**
> — Robert Fisher, Teaching Children to Learn

Reflect on this analogy: If we wanted to teach our students to catch and throw, we could bring in one tennis ball and take turns throwing it to each student and having them throw it back to us. Alternatively, we could bring in twenty balls and have our students form small groups and have them toss the ball back and forth to each other. Picture the two classrooms: One with twenty balls being caught at any one moment, and the other with just one. In which class would students better and more quickly learn to catch and throw?

The same is true with thinking skills. When we make our students more active participants in the learning process, they are given dramatically more opportunities to produce their own thought and to strengthen their own thinking skills. Would you rather have one question being asked and answered at any one moment in your class, or twenty? Small groups mean more questioning and more thinking. Instead of rarely answering a teacher question or rarely generating their own question, asking and answering questions becomes a regular part of your students' day. It is through cooperative interaction that we truly turn our classroom into a higher-level think tank. The associated personal and social benefits are invaluable.

When?
When do I use higher-level thinking questions?

Do I use these questions at the beginning of the lesson, during the lesson, or after? The answer, of course, is all of the above.

Use these questions or your own thinking questions at the beginning of the lesson to provide a motivational set for the lesson. Pique students' interest about the content with some provocative questions: "What would happen if we didn't have gravity?" "Why did Pilgrims get along with some Native Americans, but not others?" "What do you think this book will be about?" Make the content personally relevant by bringing in students' own knowledge, experiences, and feelings about the content: "What do you know about spiders?" "What things do you like about mystery stories?" "How would you feel if explorers invaded your land and killed your family?" "What do you wonder about electricity?"

Use the higher-level thinking questions throughout your lessons. Use the many questions and activities in this book not as a replacement of your curriculum, but as an additional avenue to explore the content and stretch students' thinking skills.

Use the questions after your lesson. Use the higher-level thinking questions, a journal writing activity, or the question starters as an extension activity to your lesson or unit.

Or just use the questions as stand-alone sponge activities for students or teams who have finished their work and need a challenging project to work on.

It doesn't matter when you use them, just use them frequently. As questioning becomes a habitual part of the classroom day, students' fear of asking silly questions is diminished. As the ancient Chinese proverb states, "Those who ask a silly question may seem a fool for five minutes, but those who do not ask remain a fool for life."

> ## The important thing is to never stop questioning.
> — Albert Einstein

As teachers, we should make a conscious effort to ensure that a portion of the many questions we ask on a daily basis are those that move our students beyond rote memorization. When we integrate higher-level thinking questions into our daily lessons, we transform our role from transmitters of knowledge to engineers of learning.

Where?
Where should I keep this book?

Keep it close by. Inside there are 16 sets of questions. Pull it out any time you teach these topics or need a quick, easy, fun activity or journal writing topic.

How?
How do I get the most out of this book?

In this book you will find 16 topics arranged alphabetically. For each topic there are reproducible pages for: 1) 16 Question Cards, 2) a Journal Writing activity page, 3) and a Question Starters activity page.

1. Question Cards

The Question Cards are truly the heart of this book. There are numerous ways the Question Cards can be used. After the other activity pages are introduced, you will find a description of a variety of engaging formats to use the Question Cards.

Specific and General Questions

Some of the questions provided in this book series are content-specific and others are content-free. For example, the literature questions in the Literature books are content-specific. Questions for the Great Kapok Tree deal specifically with that literature selection. Some language arts questions in the Language Arts book, on the other hand, are content-free. They are general questions that can be used over and over again with new content. For example, the Book Review questions can be used after reading any book. The Story Structure questions can be used after reading any story. You can tell by glancing at the title of the set and some of the questions whether the set is content-specific or content-free.

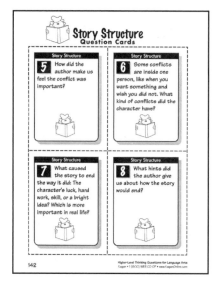

A Little Disclaimer

Not all of the "questions" on the Question Cards are actually questions. Some instruct students to do something. For example, "Compare and contrast…" We can also use these directives to develop the various facets of students' thinking skills.

The Power of Think Time

As you and your students use these questions, don't forget about the power of Think Time! There are two different think times. The first is the time between the question and the response. The second is the time between the response and feedback on the response. Think time has been shown to greatly enhance the quality of student thinking. If students are not pausing for either think time, or doing it too briefly, emphasize its importance. Five little seconds of silent think time after the question and five more seconds before feedback are proven, powerful ways to promote higher-level thinking in your class.

Use Your Question Cards for Years

For attractive Question Cards that will last for years, photocopy them on color card-stock paper and laminate them. To save time, have the Materials Monitor from each team pick up one card set, a pair of scissors for the team, and an envelope or rubber band. Each team cuts out their own set of Question Cards. When they are done with the activity, students can place the Question Cards in the envelope and write the name of the set on the envelope or wrap the cards with a rubber band for storage.

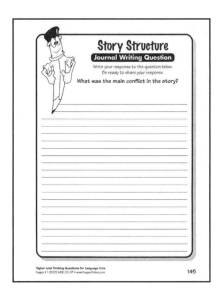

2. Journal Question

The Journal Writing page contains one of the 16 questions as a journal writing prompt. You can substitute any question, or use one of your own. The power of journal writing cannot be overstated. The act of writing takes longer than speaking and thinking. It allows the brain time to make deep connections to the content. Writing requires the writer to present his or her response in a clear, concise language. Writing develops both strong thinking and communication skills.

A helpful activity before journal writing is to have students discuss the question in pairs or in small teams. Students discuss their ideas and what they plan to write. This little prewriting activity ignites ideas for those students who stare blankly at their Journal Writing page. The interpersonal interaction further helps students articulate what they are thinking about the topic and invites students to delve deeper into the topic.

Tell students before they write that they will share their journal entries with a partner or with their team. This motivates many students to improve their entry. Sharing written responses also promotes flexible thinking with open-ended questions, and allows students to hear their peers' responses, ideas and writing styles.

Have students keep a collection of their journal entries in a three-ring binder. This way you can collect them if you wish for assessment or have students go back to reflect on their own learning. If you are using questions across the curriculum, each subject can have its own journal or own section within the binder. Use the provided blackline on the following page for a cover for students' journals or have students design their own.

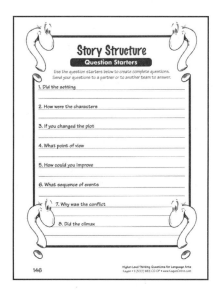

3. Question Starters

The Question Starters activity page is designed to put the questions in the hands of your students. Use these question starters to scaffold your students' ability to write their own thinking questions. This page includes eight question starters to direct students to generate questions across the levels and types of thinking. This Question Starters activity page can be used in a few different ways:

Individual Questions

Have students independently come up with their own questions. When done, they can trade their questions with a partner. On a separate sheet of paper students answer their partners' questions. After answering, partners can share how they answered each other's questions.

JOURNAL

My Best Thinking

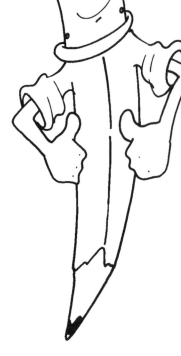

_____

This Journal Belongs to

Higher-Level Thinking Questions for Language Arts
Kagan • 1 (800) 933-2667 • www.KaganOnline.com

Pair Questions

Students work in pairs to generate questions to send to another pair. Partners take turns writing each question and also take turns recording each answer. After answering, pairs pair up to share how they answered each other's questions.

Team Questions

Students work in teams to generate questions to send to another team. Teammates take turns writing each question and recording each answer. After answering, teams pair up to share how they answered each other's questions.

Teacher-Led Questions

For young students, lead the whole class in coming up with good higher-level thinking questions.

Teach Your Students About Thinking and Questions

An effective tool to improve students' thinking skills is to teach students about the types of thinking skills and types of questions. Teaching students about the types of thinking skills improves their metacognitive abilities. When students are aware of the types of thinking, they may more effectively plan, monitor, and evaluate their own thinking. When students understand the types of questions and the basics of question construction, they are more likely to create effective higher-level thinking questions. In doing so they develop their own thinking skills and the thinking of classmates as they work to answer each other's questions.

Table of Activities

The Question Cards can be used in a variety of game-like formats to forge students' thinking skills. They can be used for cooperative team and pair work, for whole-class questioning, for independent activities, or at learning centers. On the following pages you will find numerous excellent options to use your Question Cards. As you use the Question Cards in this book, try the different activities listed below to add novelty and variety to the higher-level thinking process.

Activities

team activity #1

Question Commander

Preferably in teams of four, students shuffle their Question Cards and place them in a stack, questions facing down, so that all teammates can easily reach the Question Cards. Give each team a Question Commander set of instructions (blackline provided on following page) to lead them through each question.

Student One becomes the Question Commander for the first question. The Question Commander reads the question aloud to the team, then asks the teammates to think about the question and how they would answer it. After the think time, the Question Commander selects a teammate to answer the question. The Question Commander can spin a spinner or roll a die to select who will answer. After the teammate gives the answer, Question Commander again calls for think time, this time asking the team to think about the answer. After the think time, the Question Commander leads a team

discussion in which any teammember can contribute his or her thoughts or ideas to the question, or give praise or reactions to the answer.

When the discussion is over, Student Two becomes the Question Commander for the next question.

Question Commander

Question Commander
Instruction Cards

Question Commander

1. Ask the Question: Question Commander reads the question to the team.

2. Think Time: "Think of your best answer."

3. Answer the Question: The Question Commander selects a teammate to answer the question.

4. Think Time: "Think about how you would answer differently or add to the answer."

5. Team Discussion: As a team, discuss other possible answers or reactions to the answer given.

Question Commander

1. Ask the Question: Question Commander reads the question to the team.

2. Think Time: "Think of your best answer."

3. Answer the Question: The Question Commander selects a teammate to answer the question.

4. Think Time: "Think about how you would answer differently or add to the answer."

5. Team Discussion: As a team, discuss other possible answers or reactions to the answer given.

Question Commander

1. Ask the Question: Question Commander reads the question to the team.

2. Think Time: "Think of your best answer."

3. Answer the Question: The Question Commander selects a teammate to answer the question.

4. Think Time: "Think about how you would answer differently or add to the answer."

5. Team Discussion: As a team, discuss other possible answers or reactions to the answer given.

Question Commander

1. Ask the Question: Question Commander reads the question to the team.

2. Think Time: "Think of your best answer."

3. Answer the Question: The Question Commander selects a teammate to answer the question.

4. Think Time: "Think about how you would answer differently or add to the answer."

5. Team Discussion: As a team, discuss other possible answers or reactions to the answer given.

Fan-N-Pick

In a team of four, Student One fans out the question cards, and says, "Pick a card, any card!" Student Two picks a card and reads the question out loud to teammates. After five seconds of think time, Student Three gives his or her answer. After another five seconds of think time, Student Four paraphrases, praises, or adds to the answer given. Students rotate roles for each new round.

Spin-N-Think

Spin-N-Think spinners are available from Kagan to lead teams through the steps of higher-level thinking. Students spin the Spin-N-Think™ spinner to select a student at each stage of the questioning to: 1) ask the question, 2) answer the question, 3) paraphrase and praise the answer, 4) augment the answer, and 5) discuss the question or answer. The Spin-N-Think™ game makes higher-level thinking more fun, and holds students accountable because they are often called upon, but never know when their number will come up.

Three-Step Interview

After the question is read to the team, students pair up. The first step is an interview in which one student interviews the other about the question. In the second step, students remain with their partner but switch roles: The interviewer becomes the interviewee. In the third step, the pairs come back together and each student in turn presents to the team what their partner shared. Three-Step Interview is strong for individual accountability, active listening, and paraphrasing skills.

Team Discussion

Team Discussion is an easy and informal way of processing the questions: Students read a question and then throw it open for discussion. Team Discussion, however, does not ensure that there is individual accountability or equal participation.

Think-Pair-Square

One student reads a question out loud to teammates. Partners on the same side of the table then pair up to discuss the question and their answers. Then, all four students come together for an open discussion about the question.

Question-Write-RoundRobin

Students take turns asking the team the question. After each question is asked, each student writes his or her ideas on a piece of paper. After students have finished writing, in turn they share their ideas. This format creates strong individual accountability because each student is expected to develop and share an answer for every question.

Mix-Pair-Discuss

Each student gets a different Question Card. For 16 to 32 students, use two sets of questions. In this case, some students may have the same question which is OK. Students get out of their seats and mix around the classroom. They pair up with a partner. One partner reads his or her Question Card and the other answers. Then they switch roles. When done they trade cards and find a new partner. The process is repeated for a predetermined amount of time. The rule is students cannot pair up with the same partner twice. Students may get the same questions twice or more, but each time it is with a new partner. This strategy is a fun, energizing way to ask and answer questions.

Think-Pair-Share

Think-Pair-Share is teacher-directed. The teacher asks the question, then gives students think time. Students then pair up to share their thoughts about the question. After the pair discussion, one student is called on to share with the class what was shared in his or her pair. Think-Pair-Share does not provide as much active participation for students as Think-Pair-Square because only one student is called upon at a time, but is a nice way to do whole-class sharing.

Inside-Outside Circle

Each student gets a Question Card. Half of the students form a circle facing out. The other half forms a circle around the inside circle; each student in the outside circle faces one student in the inside circle. Students in the outside circle ask inside circle students a question. After the inside circle students answer the question, students switch roles questioning and answering. After both have asked and answered a question, they each praise the other's answers and then hold up a hand indicating they are finished. When most students have a hand up, have students trade cards with their partner and rotate to a new partner. To rotate, tell the outside circle to move to the left. This format is a lively and enjoyable way to ask questions and have students listen to the thinking of many classmates.

Question & Answer

This might sound familiar: Instead of giving students the Question Cards, the teacher asks the questions and calls on one student at a time to answer. This traditional format eliminates simultaneous, cooperative interaction, but may be good for introducing younger students to higher-level questions.

Numbered Heads Together

Students number off in their teams so that every student has a number. The teacher asks a question. Students put their "heads together" to discuss the question. The teacher then calls on a number and selects a student with that number to share what his or her team discussed.

pair activity #1

RallyRobin

Each pair gets a set of Question Cards. Student A in the pair reads the question out loud to his or her partner. Student B answers. Partners take turns asking and answering each question.

Pair Discussion

Partners take turns asking the question. The pair then discusses the answer together. Unlike RallyRobin, students discuss the answer. Both students contribute to answering and to discussing each other's ideas.

Question-Write-Share-Discuss

One partner reads the Question Card out loud to his or her teammate. Both students write down their ideas. Partners take turns sharing what they wrote. Partners discuss how their ideas are similar and different.

Journal Writing

Students pick one Question Card and make a journal entry or use the question as the prompt for an essay or creative writing. Have students share their writing with a partner or in turn with teammates.

Independent Answers

Students each get their own set of Questions Cards. Pairs or teams can share a set of questions, or the questions can be written on the board or put on the overhead projector. Students work by themselves to answer the questions on a separate sheet of paper. When done, students can compare their answers with a partner, teammates, or the whole class.

Center Ideas

1. Question Card Center

At one center, have the Question Cards and a Spin-N-Think™ spinner, Question Commander instruction card, or Fan-N-Pick instructions. Students lead themselves through the thinking questions. For individual accountability, have each student record their own answer for each question.

2. Journal Writing Center

At a second center, have a Journal Writing activity page for each student. Students can discuss the question with others at their center, then write their own journal entry. After everyone is done writing, students share what they wrote with other students at their center.

3. Question Starters Center

At a third center, have a Question Starters page. Split the students at the center into two groups. Have both groups create thinking questions using the Question Starters activity page. When the groups are done writing their questions, they trade questions with the other group at their center. When done answering each other's questions, two groups pair up to compare their answers.

Adventure Stories

higher-level thinking questions

"Judge of a man by his questions rather than by his answers.

— Voltaire

Adventure Stories
Question Cards

Adventure Stories

1 Are there any animals in the story? Are they important to the adventure? What kind of animal could you add?

Adventure Stories

2 What is the most memorable adventure you have had?

Adventure Stories

3 What is your favorite moment in the story?

Adventure Stories

4 Name your favorite adventure story or movie. Is there some element from that story that could be added to this story?

Adventure Stories
Question Cards

Adventure Stories

5 How many main characters were in the story? Who were they? If you were the author which character would you make most important?

Adventure Stories

6 Would you like to have an adventure like the one in the story? Tell why.

Adventure Stories

7 What was the most important event in the adventure? Why?

Adventure Stories

8 Can you think of a setting for this adventure that could be more exciting?

Higher-Level Thinking Questions for Language Arts
Kagan • 1 (800) 933-2667 • www.KaganOnline.com

Adventure Stories
Question Cards

Adventure Stories

9 What changes would you make in the story if it took place in ancient times or in the future?

Adventure Stories

10 Describe how your most memorable adventure was similar to or different from this story.

Adventure Stories

11 If this story were going to be a movie — which character would you like to play in the movie? Why?

Adventure Stories

12 Tell the author the strongest and weakest part of his story.

Adventure Stories
Question Cards

Adventure Stories

13 Did the adventure end the way you expected? Why or why not?

Adventure Stories

14 Pretend you are the author — describe another ending to the story.

Adventure Stories

15 You are the author and your job is to revise the story. How would you make it more exciting?

Adventure Stories

16 If you were going to break this story into four chapters, what would the four chapters be?

Higher-Level Thinking Questions for Language Arts
Kagan • 1 (800) 933-2667 • www.KaganOnline.com

Adventure Stories

Journal Writing Question

Write your response to the question below.
Be ready to share your response.

What is the most memorable adventure you have had?

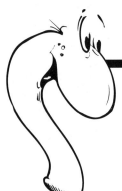

Adventure Stories

Question Starters

Use the question starters below to create complete questions.
Send your questions to a partner or to another team to answer.

1. How would you decide between

_____

_____

2. What is another way

_____

_____

3. If you were a character in the story

_____

_____

4. What would have been different if

_____

_____

5. What makes

_____

_____

6. What did you like about

_____

_____

7. If you had a similar adventure

_____

_____

8. How could you draw

_____

_____

Higher-Level Thinking Questions for Language Arts
Kagan • 1 (800) 933-2667 • www.KaganOnline.com

Book Review

higher-level thinking questions

In teaching it is the method and not the content that is the message... the drawing out, not the pumping in.

— Ashley Montague

Book Review
Question Cards

Book Review

1 What could have happened to change the outcome of the story?

Book Review

2 If the action in the story were a body of water, what kind would it be: a rushing river, a trickling creek, a calm lake, or rough seas?

Book Review

3 If the ending of the book were a dessert, what might it be?

Book Review

4 What part of the story would you change if possible? Explain your choice.

Book Review
Question Cards

Book Review

5 How did the author use imagery to create a feeling in the reader?

Book Review

6 What symbol would you choose to represent the main character's personality?

Book Review

7 Imagine yourself being interviewed as the author of the book. What would you say were your reasons for writing the book?

Book Review

8 Which character do you most closely identify with and why?

Higher-Level Thinking Questions for Language Arts
Kagan • 1 (800) 933-2667 • www.KaganOnline.com

Book Review
Question Cards

Book Review

9 What might another possible title be and why?

Book Review

10 In what other time period could this story have taken place? What would change because of it?

Book Review

11 If you were to write a critique of this book, what would the headline say?

Book Review

12 Which character do you most strongly disagree with or disapprove of and why?

Book Review
Question Cards

Book Review

13 What might a slogan say to advertise the book?

Book Review

14 If the beginning of the book were an appetizer what might it be?

Book Review

15 What is the moral of the story and why?

Book Review

16 What *do you* think is the main problem in the story? Were you satisfied with the solution? Why or why not?

Higher-Level Thinking Questions for Language Arts
Kagan • 1 (800) 933-2667 • www.KaganOnline.com

Book Review

Journal Writing Question

Write your response to the question below.
Be ready to share your response.

What is the moral of the story and why?

_____

_____

_____

_____

_____

_____

_____

_____

_____

_____

_____

_____

_____

_____

_____

_____

_____

_____

_____

_____

_____

Book Review

Use the question starters below to create complete questions.
Send your questions to a partner or to another team to answer.

1. What part of the book

2. What would have happened if

3. How did the setting

4. What symbol

5. How could you improve

6. If you were a critic

7. What do you think about

8. How could you summarize

Higher-Level Thinking Questions for Language Arts
Kagan • 1 (800) 933-2667 • www.KaganOnline.com

Fantasy
Stories

higher-level thinking questions

"Life is amazing, and the teacher had better prepare himself to be a medium for that amazement."

— Edward Blishen

Fantasy Stories
Question Cards

Fantasy Stories

1 Are there opposing forces in the story? If so, what are they?

Fantasy Stories

2 If you could be a character in the story, who would you be and why?

Fantasy Stories

3 If you had been a part of the story, and had one special power, how would you use it?

Fantasy Stories

4 What do you feel is a major problem faced by the main character?

Fantasy Stories
Question Cards

Fantasy Stories

5 What special traits or powers do the characters have that we do not?

Fantasy Stories

6 What did you enjoy most and least in this fantasy? Why?

Fantasy Stories

7 How is the world in this story like or unlike our world, and why?

Fantasy Stories

8 How has the author made the story believable?

Fantasy Stories
Question Cards

Fantasy Stories

9 What is your favorite part of the story? Why?

Fantasy Stories

10 What stories have you read that are similar to this one?

Fantasy Stories

11 At what point did you have the most intense feelings? Why?

Fantasy Stories

12 If you were an artist, how would you illustrate this book differently?

Fantasy Stories
Question Cards

Fantasy Stories

13 Have you ever felt like one of the characters in the story? When and why?

Fantasy Stories

14 Explain two different ways to solve the problem in the story.

Fantasy Stories

15 What is the least believable part of the story? How could you make it more believable?

Fantasy Stories

16 Describe what you think the author looks like.

Higher-Level Thinking Questions for Language Arts
Kagan • 1 (800) 933-2667 • www.KaganOnline.com

Fantasy Stories

Journal Writing Question

Write your response to the question below.
Be ready to share your response.

What is your favorite part of the story? Why?

_____

_____

_____

_____

_____

_____

_____

_____

_____

_____

_____

_____

_____

_____

_____

_____

_____

_____

_____

_____

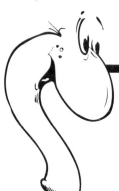

Fantasy Stories

Question Starters

Use the question starters below to create complete questions.
Send your questions to a partner or to another team to answer.

1. Why is this story

2. Can you relate

3. If you were the author

4. What would have happened if

5. What part of the story

6. In your own life

7. How might you change

8. What is the relationship between

Higher-Level Thinking Questions for Language Arts
Kagan • 1 (800) 933-2667 • www.KaganOnline.com

Mystery Stories

higher-level thinking questions

"The only reason some people get lost in thought is because it's unfamiliar territory.

— Paul Fix

Mystery Stories
Question Cards

Mystery Stories

1 Which character in the book would you most like to be? Why?

Mystery Stories

2 Did you think the events in the book could really happen? Why?

Mystery Stories

3 If you were going to write a mystery story, where would the setting be?

Mystery Stories

4 Was the setting crucial to the mystery?

Mystery Stories

5 What clues did the author give to help you solve the mystery?

Mystery Stories

6 How did the author build your suspense?

Mystery Stories

7 Did you solve the mystery before it was solved in the book? If so, how did you do it?

Mystery Stories

8 Did the author throw you off track? If so, how? If not, why not?

Higher-Level Thinking Questions for Language Arts
Kagan • 1 (800) 933-2667 • www.KaganOnline.com

Mystery Stories
Question Cards

Mystery Stories

9 What part of the book did you enjoy most?

Mystery Stories

10 Name a TV program or movie most like this story. Why?

Mystery Stories

11 Were there any characters you could eliminate or change?

Mystery Stories

12 Tell your teammates some things about the main character the author forgot to tell us.

Mystery Stories

13 Did you enjoy the ending? Why or why not?

Mystery Stories

14 Pretend you are the author — how could you create more suspense?

Mystery Stories

15 Describe a moment when you changed your mind about what was going to happen.

Mystery Stories

16 If this story took place in the year 2050, what are some of the changes you would have to make?

Mystery Stories
Journal Writing Question

Write your response to the question below.
Be ready to share your response.

What clues did the author give to help you solve the mystery?

_____

_____

_____

_____

_____

_____

_____

_____

_____

_____

_____

_____

_____

_____

_____

_____

_____

_____

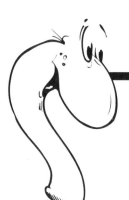

Mystery Stories
Question Starters

Use the question starters below to create complete questions.
Send your questions to a partner or to another team to answer.

1. How can you explain

2. What part of the story

3. Which character

4. How could you make the story

5. If you were in the story

6. What was the importance of

7. Would you rather

8. How is this story like

Higher-Level Thinking Questions for Language Arts
Kagan • 1 (800) 933-2667 • www.KaganOnline.com

Oral
Presentation
Preparation

higher-level thinking questions

"The whole art of teaching is only the art of awakening the natural curiosity of young minds...

— Anatole France

Oral Presentation
Question Cards

1 To whom will you be speaking and what will interest them?

2 This topic is like_____ because_____.

3 What might a slogan be to help others remember your topic?

4 How can I change the sound of my voice to make my presentation more interesting?

Oral Presentation
Question Cards

Oral Presentation

5 What symbol could you display to represent your topic?

Oral Presentation

6 What do you already know about this topic?

Oral Presentation

7 What do you need to learn about the topic?

Oral Presentation

8 What might be the opening sentence of your presentation?

Higher-Level Thinking Questions for Language Arts
Kagan • 1 (800) 933-2667 • www.KaganOnline.com

Oral Presentation
Question Cards

Oral Presentation

9 What might you say to close your presentation?

Oral Presentation

10 What are your main points?

Oral Presentation

11 What are the facts/opinions about your topic?

Oral Presentation

12 How can gestures and movement make the presentation more interesting?

Oral Presentation
Question Cards

Oral Presentation

13 How might you use a graph or chart in your presentation?

Oral Presentation

14 What questions might you ask of your audience?

Oral Presentation

15 Why is the topic important?

Oral Presentation

16 What would you like people to remember about your topic?

Higher-Level Thinking Questions for Language Arts
Kagan • 1 (800) 933-2667 • www.KaganOnline.com

Oral Presentation

Journal Writing Question

Write your response to the question below.
Be ready to share your response.

How do you plan to grab your audience's attention and keep it throughout your presentation?

_____

_____

_____

_____

_____

_____

_____

_____

_____

_____

_____

_____

_____

_____

_____

_____

_____

Oral Presentation

Question Starters

Use the question starters below to create complete questions.
Send your questions to a partner or to another team to answer.

1. What music might

2. How might visual aids

3. Will your audience

4. How do you feel about

5. Do you think your topic

6. What information

7. If you were in the audience

8. What other senses can you

Higher-Level Thinking Questions for Language Arts
Kagan • 1 (800) 933-2667 • www.KaganOnline.com

Poetry
Possibilities

higher-level thinking questions

"No man really becomes a fool until he stops asking questions.

— Charles Steinmetz

Poetry Possibilities
Question Cards

Poetry Possibilities

1 If this poem were to be set to music, what type of instruments could be used?

Poetry Possibilities

2 What is another possible title for the poem?

Poetry Possibilities

3 If the poem inspired a TV show, what type of show would it be: a comedy, an action/adventure or a drama, and why?

Poetry Possibilities

4 What do you think the author was trying to say through the poem?

Poetry Possibilities
Question Cards

5 Poetry often creates an emotional response in the reader. Choose one word to represent your response.

6 Why *do you* think the author chose to rhyme or not rhyme the poem?

7 If the poem were a flower, would it be a thorny rose, a delicate tulip, a wild poppy, or a (choose your own) _____?

8 Imagine the poem written on the inside of a greeting card. Describe the picture on the front of the card.

Higher-Level Thinking Questions for Language Arts
Kagan Publishing • 1 (800) 933-2667 • www.KaganOnline.com

Poetry Possibilities
Question Cards

Poetry Possibilities

9 Imagine this poem as a book and describe the main character.

Poetry Possibilities

10 What do you think the author was doing immediately before writing the poem?

Poetry Possibilities

11 Choose one word to describe the rhythm of the poem.

Poetry Possibilities

12 How might a reader have felt about the poem 100 years ago? Why?

Poetry Possibilities
Question Cards

Poetry Possibilities

13 Suggest to the author a way to improve his or her poem.

Poetry Possibilities

14 To whom do you imagine the author was writing and why?

Poetry Possibilities

15 How do you think the author was feeling as he or she wrote the poem?

Poetry Possibilities

16 Will the poem make sense 100 years in the future? Explain your answer.

Higher-Level Thinking Questions for Language Arts
Kagan Publishing • 1 (800) 933-2667 • www.KaganOnline.com

Poetry Possibilities

Journal Writing Question

Write your response to the question below.
Be ready to share your response.

Imagine the poem written on the inside of a greeting card. Describe the picture on the front of the card.

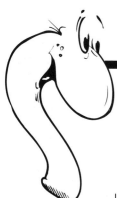

Poetry Possibilities

Question Starters

Use the question starters below to create complete questions.
Send your questions to a partner or to another team to answer.

1. If you wrote the poem

2. What part of the poem

3. In which line

4. What does the style

5. What is the meaning of

6. In your opinion,

7. What effect does

8. What makes this poem

Higher-Level Thinking Questions for Language Arts
Kagan • 1 (800) 933-2667 • www.KaganOnline.com

Prewriting:
Biography/ Autobiography

higher-level thinking questions

"All the resources we need are in the mind."

— Theodore Roosevelt

Prewriting: Biography/Autobiography
Question Cards

Prewriting: Biography/Autobiography

1 How might you organize the information to show the emotional, intellectual, and physical growth of the subject?

Prewriting: Biography/Autobiography

2 What do you consider to be your subject's greatest accomplishment? Explain your choice.

Prewriting: Biography/Autobiography

3 How is the physical description of your subject important to his/her life story?

Prewriting: Biography/Autobiography

4 For what single action will the subject be most remembered?

Prewriting: Biography/Autobiography
Question Cards

Prewriting: Biography/Autobiography

5 How can you best portray the highlight in the life of your subject?

Prewriting: Biography/Autobiography

6 What *do you* consider to be your subject's greatest strength and greatest weakness? Why?

Prewriting: Biography/Autobiography

7 What might be changed if your subject did not exist?

Prewriting: Biography/Autobiography

8 What *do the* actions of the subject tell you about his morals and values?

Higher-Level Thinking Questions for Language Arts
Kagan • 1 (800) 933-2667 • www.KaganOnline.com

Prewriting: Biography/Autobiography
Question Cards

Prewriting: Biography/Autobiography

9 What descriptive words might you use to describe the personality of your subject?

Prewriting: Biography/Autobiography

10 Choose a symbol to represent your subject. Explain your choice.

Prewriting: Biography/Autobiography

11 What *do you* think was your subject's biggest challenge?

Prewriting: Biography/Autobiography

12 If the subject had lived his or her life in a different country, what may have been different?

Prewriting: Biography/Autobiography
Question Cards

Prewriting: Biography/Autobiography

13 Complete the following statement. The subject is like_____ because_____.

Prewriting: Biography/Autobiography

14 Who do you think had the greatest impact on your subject? Why?

Prewriting: Biography/Autobiography

15 Culture plays a big part in who we are. What part does the cultural background of the subject play in his or her life?

Prewriting: Biography/Autobiography

16 What slogan might you use to best advertise this life story?

Higher-Level Thinking Questions for Language Arts
Kagan • 1 (800) 933-2667 • www.KaganOnline.com

Prewriting: Biography/ Autobiography

Journal Writing Question

Write your response to the question below.
Be ready to share your response.

What do you consider to be your subject's greatest accomplishment? Explain your choice.

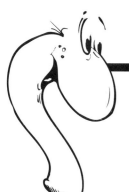

Prewriting: Biography/ Autobiography

Question Starters

Use the question starters below to create complete questions.
Send your questions to a partner or to another team to answer.

1. How might you sequence

2. What is the most important

3. How do you feel about

4. What event

5. What might the reader think if

6. How could you describe

7. What is the relationship

8. What is the best

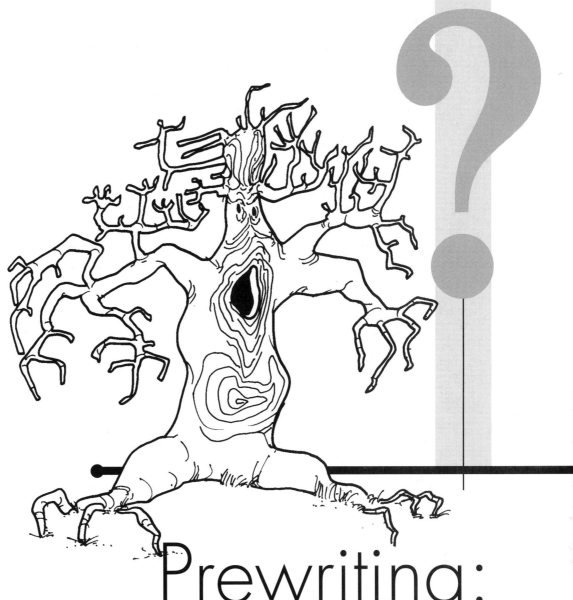

Prewriting:
Mysteries

higher-level thinking questions

"Never express yourself more clearly than you are able to think.

— Niels Bohr

Prewriting: Mysteries
Question Cards

Prewriting: Mysteries

1 How will you use foreshadowing in your story?

Prewriting: Mysteries

2 How will you capture the reader's attention in the beginning of the story?

Prewriting: Mysteries

3 What characteristics might the main character have that will add to the mystery of the story?

Prewriting: Mysteries

4 How will you build suspense in the story?

Prewriting: Mysteries
Question Cards

Prewriting: Mysteries

5 Will the reader know more about the mystery than the characters? Explain your choice.

Prewriting: Mysteries

6 How will the mystery be resolved?

Prewriting: Mysteries

7 How will the setting add to the mystery of the story?

Prewriting: Mysteries

8 How would you like the reader to feel at the end of the story?

Higher-Level Thinking Questions for Language Arts
Kagan • 1 (800) 933-2667 • www.KaganOnline.com

Prewriting: Mysteries
Question Cards

Prewriting: Mysteries

9 Explain why you have chosen to include/exclude a hero/heroine.

Prewriting: Mysteries

10 What words can you use to describe the action in the story?

Prewriting: Mysteries

11 What clues can you give the reader to reveal the mysterious plot?

Prewriting: Mysteries

12 Share a possible title for your story.

Prewriting: Mysteries

13 Might there be a crime in the story. Why or why not?

Prewriting: Mysteries

14 Which event will be the climax of the story?

Prewriting: Mysteries

15 What events lead up to the climax in the story?

Prewriting: Mysteries

16 Will one of the characters tell the story or will there be an observer/narrator?

Prewriting: Mysteries

Journal Writing Question

Write your response to the question below.
Be ready to share your response.

How will you capture the reader's attention in the beginning of the story?

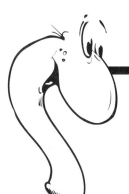

Prewriting: Mysteries
Question Starters

Use the question starters below to create complete questions.
Send your questions to a partner or to another team to answer.

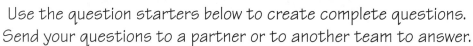

1. When the reader reads your story,

2. How will your characters

3. How will your climax

4. What symbols

5. Will foreshadowing

6. What mysterious things

7. How will you

8. How will your climax

Higher-Level Thinking Questions for Language Arts
Kagan • 1 (800) 933-2667 • www.KaganOnline.com

Prewriting:
Persuasive Writing

higher-level thinking questions

Men fear thought as they fear nothing else on earth more than ruin more even than death. Thought is subversive and revolutionary, destructive and terrible, thought is merciless to privilege, established institutions, and comfortable habit. Thought looks into the pit of hell and is not afraid. Thought is great and swift and free, the light of the world, and the chief glory of man.

— Bertrand Russell

Prewriting: Persuasive Writing
Question Cards

Persuasive Writing

1 Name three strong/vivid words to describe your topic?

Persuasive Writing

2 Why should your reader agree with you?

Persuasive Writing

3 How might you convince your reader to believe you?

Persuasive Writing

4 What are the good points about your topic?

Prewriting: Persuasive Writing
Question Cards

Persuasive Writing
5 What do you want people to know about your topic?

Persuasive Writing
6 How might you begin your piece to "grab" the reader?

Persuasive Writing
7 What might a catchy title be for your piece?

Persuasive Writing
8 How would you like your reader to feel about your topic?

Higher-Level Thinking Questions for Language Arts
Kagan • 1 (800) 933-2667 • www.KaganOnline.com

Prewriting: Persuasive Writing
Question Cards

Persuasive Writing

9 What are some possible arguments against your topic?

Persuasive Writing

10 Where can you find information about your topic?

Persuasive Writing

11 Can you quote some experts on the topic?

Persuasive Writing

12 What kinds of information will make your writing stronger?

Prewriting: Persuasive Writing
Question Cards

Persuasive Writing

13 What are the most important points?

Persuasive Writing

14 Is there information you'd like to leave out and why?

Persuasive Writing

15 What are the facts that back up your opinion?

Persuasive Writing

16 What will you say to give your piece a strong ending?

Higher-Level Thinking Questions for Language Arts
Kagan • 1 (800) 933-2667 • www.KaganOnline.com

Prewriting:
Persuasive Writing

Journal Writing Question

Write your response to the question below.
Be ready to share your response.

How do you plan to persuade your reader?

_____

_____

_____

_____

_____

_____

_____

_____

_____

_____

_____

_____

_____

_____

_____

_____

_____

_____

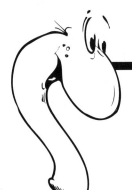

Prewriting: Persuasive Writing

Question Starters

Use the question starters below to create complete questions.
Send your questions to a partner or to another team to answer.

1. What arguments will you

_____

2. If you were making a commercial

_____

3. How will you persuade

_____

4. What kind of information

_____

5. What is the strongest

_____

6. Will convincing others

_____

7. How will readers

_____

8. If you read your own writing

_____

Higher-Level Thinking Questions for Language Arts
Kagan • 1 (800) 933-2667 • www.KaganOnline.com

Prewriting:
Stories

higher-level thinking questions

The most beautiful thing in the world is, precisely, the conjunction of learning and inspiration. Oh, the joy of discovery!

— Wanda Landowska

Prewriting: Stories
Question Cards

Prewriting: Stories

1 How might you let the reader know about your main character's personality?

Prewriting: Stories

2 The relationship between characters is very important to a story. With whom might be the main character's most important relationship?

Prewriting: Stories

3 What are two possible solutions to the main problem in the story?

Prewriting: Stories

4 What might be the moral to your story?

Prewriting: Stories
Question Cards

5 In what area would your story most likely take place? What clues can you use to let the reader know about the setting?

6 How could the weather play a part in your story?

7 Which character might best tell the story and why?

8 How do you hope the ending will make the reader feel?

Higher-Level Thinking Questions for Language Arts
Kagan • 1 (800) 933-2667 • www.KaganOnline.com

Prewriting: Stories
Question Cards

Prewriting: Stories

9 How might you best capture the reader's attention at the beginning of the story?

Prewriting: Stories

10 What hints could you use to let the reader know how the story might end?

Prewriting: Stories

11 When will the action in the story climax? Explain your reasoning.

Prewriting: Stories

12 What could you call your story?

Prewriting: Stories

13 How will the plot develop? What will happen first, second...

Prewriting: Stories

14 What will be the main problem or conflict in your story?

Prewriting: Stories

15 What is your character's motive? Why does he or she do the things he or she does?

Prewriting: Stories

16 How might you illustrate your story?

Prewriting: Stories

Journal Writing Question

Write your response to the question below.
Be ready to share your response.

When will the action in the story climax?
Explain your reasoning.

Prewriting: Stories
Question Starters

Use the question starters below to create complete questions.
Send your questions to a partner or to another team to answer.

1. How will your characters

2. What *do you hope*

3. How will you illustrate

4. What will the setting

5. How will you sequence

6. Will the conflict

7. Where in the story will you

8. Will your main character

Higher-Level Thinking Questions for Language Arts
Kagan • 1 (800) 933-2667 • www.KaganOnline.com

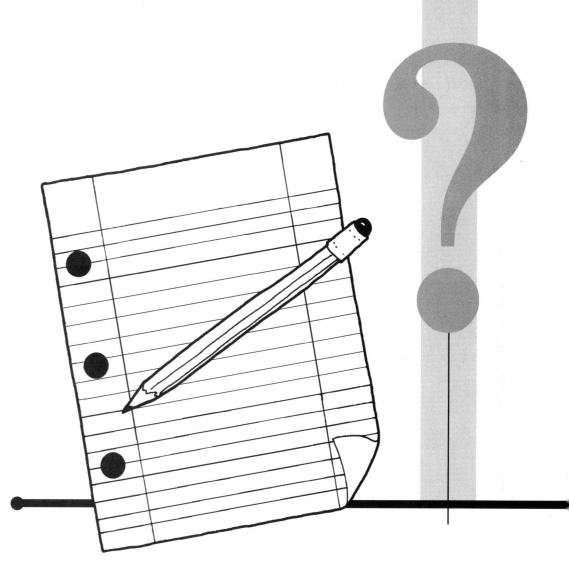

Self-Editing

higher-level thinking questions

"Man's greatness lies in his power of thought.

— Blaise Pascal

Self-Editing
Question Cards

Self-Editing

1 Have I said what I was trying to say?

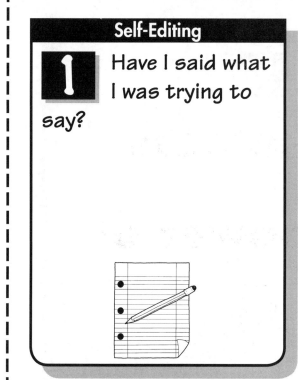

Self-Editing

2 What is the most exciting or strongest part ?

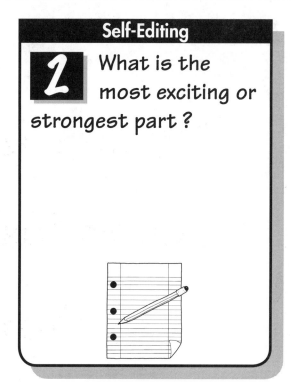

Self-Editing

3 Does this piece need more or less conversation?

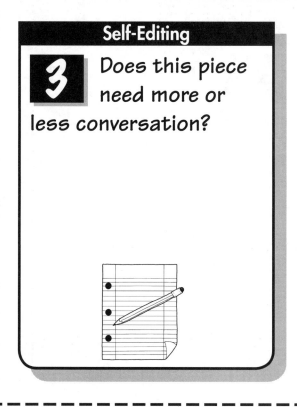

Self-Editing

4 Are there parts that don't fit with the topic?

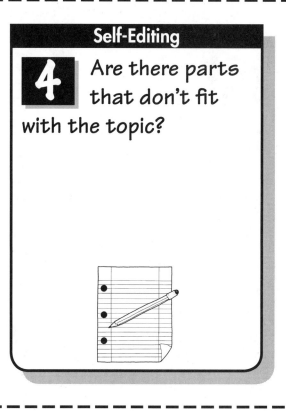

Self-Editing
Question Cards

Self-Editing

5 Does my title fit with what I've written?

Self-Editing

6 Does my first sentence and paragraph "grab" the reader?

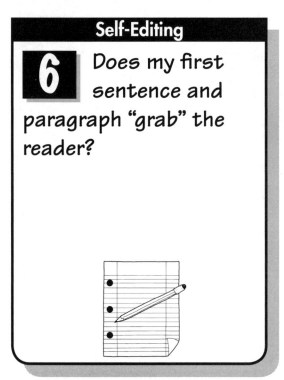

Self-Editing

7 Have I used any words too often?

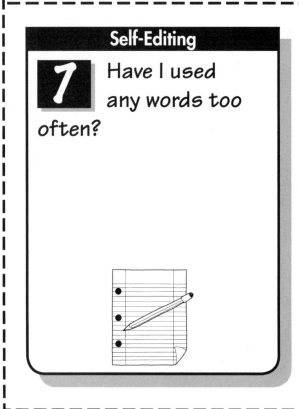

Self-Editing

8 Are my sentences too long?

Self-Editing
Question Cards

Self-Editing

9 Have I organized my ideas into paragraphs?

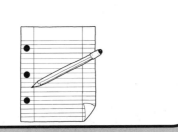

Self-Editing

10 Is my information in order?

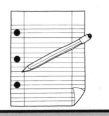

Self-Editing

11 Who is telling this story? Does it stay the same all through the piece?

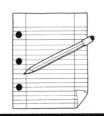

Self-Editing

12 How does the setting add to the piece?

Self-Editing
Question Cards

13 Have I "wrapped up" the information or story at the end?

14 Have I spelled every word correctly?

15 Have I used correct punctuation and capitalization?

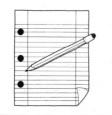

16 Have I described the information well enough that the reader can "see" what I mean?

Self-Editing

Journal Writing Question

Write your response to the question below.
Be ready to share your response.

What are the strengths of your writing?
What would you like to improve?

Self-Editing

Question Starters

Use the question starters below to create complete questions.
Send your questions to a partner or to another team to answer.

1. How would you grade

2. What improvements

3. What was the most difficult

4. Did you like

5. How do you feel

6. If you were going to start again

7. What is your favorite

8. What do you think your teacher

Higher-Level Thinking Questions for Language Arts
Kagan • 1 (800) 933-2667 • www.KaganOnline.com

Story
Characters

higher-level thinking questions

"Quality questions create a quality life. Successful people ask better questions, and as a result, they get better answers.

— Anthony Robbins

Story Characters
Question Cards

Story Characters

1 What did the main character do to make you like or dislike him or her?

Story Characters

2 What is a color that describes the main character? Why?

Story Characters

3 What can you say about the main character's family life?

Story Characters

4 When did you face a problem in your life like one faced by the character?

Story Characters
Question Cards

5 How is the role of the supporting character or characters important to the story?

6 How did the character change or grow from the beginning to the end?

7 Why is the main character like you or unlike you?

8 Who did the character go to for support and understanding? Who could the character go to?

Higher-Level Thinking Questions for Language Arts
Kagan • 1 (800) 933-2667 • www.KaganOnline.com

Story Characters
Question Cards

Story Characters

9 What would happen if the main character was a different sex or a different species?

Story Characters

10 What might the main character have done in the beginning to change the story outcome?

Story Characters

11 What will happen to the character in a sequel to the book?

Story Characters

12 Where will the main character be 20 years from now?

Story Characters
Question Cards

Story Characters

13 Who might be able to replace the main character? Pick a character from an animated show.

Story Characters

14 How might you describe the character to a blind person?

Story Characters

15 Why would you want to be the character's friend? If not, why not?

Story Characters

16 How would the character be different if the story were fiction or nonfiction?

Higher-Level Thinking Questions for Language Arts
Kagan • 1 (800) 933-2667 • www.KaganOnline.com

Story Characters

Journal Writing Question

Write your response to the question below.
Be ready to share your response.

How did the character change or grow from the beginning to the end?

Story Characters
Question Starters

Use the question starters below to create complete questions.
Send your questions to a partner or to another team to answer.

1. If you were the main character

2. If this book was a movie,

3. What was the relationship between

4. How could you describe the personality of

5. How would the story be different if

6. What if all the characters

7. How is the main character like

8. What symbol best represents

Higher-Level Thinking Questions for Language Arts
Kagan • 1 (800) 933-2667 • www.KaganOnline.com

Story Plot

higher-level thinking questions

"The uncreative mind can spot wrong answers, but it takes a very creative mind to spot wrong questions.

— Anthony Jay

Higher-Level Thinking Questions for Language Arts
Kagan • 1 (800) 933-2667 • www.KaganOnline.com

Story Plot
Question Cards

Story Plot

1 How does the author capture the reader's attention in the beginning of the story?

Story Plot

2 What part of the plot did you like the best? Share your reasons.

Story Plot

3 What one word would you use to describe the plot? Why?

Story Plot

4 What would the sequel to the story be?

Story Plot
Question Cards

Story Plot

5 When in the story does the action climax?

Story Plot

6 How does the age of the main character(s) influence his or her actions?

Story Plot

7 Why did the author end the story as he or she did?

Story Plot

8 What events in the story could happen to you?

Higher-Level Thinking Questions for Language Arts
Kagan • 1 (800) 933-2667 • www.KaganOnline.com

Story Plot

9 How does the setting effect the action in the story?

Story Plot

10 How might changing a major event affect the outcome of the story?

Story Plot

11 Give another ending for the story without changing the plot.

Story Plot

12 Which single event had the greatest impact on the outcome? Why?

Story Plot
Question Cards

Story Plot

13 What do you think is the main problem in the story?

Story Plot

14 What does the action in the story remind you of...a roller-coaster ride, a leisurely stroll, a river rafting trip, or a _____? Why?

Story Plot

15 Where in the story did you feel the most intense emotion? Why did that part bring about emotion?

Story Plot

16 What other story are you reminded of?

Higher-Level Thinking Questions for Language Arts
Kagan • 1 (800) 933-2667 • www.KaganOnline.com

Story Plot

Journal Writing Question

Write your response to the question below.
Be ready to share your response.

What would the sequel to the story be?

Story Plot
Question Starters

Use the question starters below to create complete questions.
Send your questions to a partner or to another team to answer.

1. How does the author

_____

_____

2. How is the setting

_____

_____

3. Why did

_____

_____

4. Do the characters in the story

_____

_____

5. In your opinion, is the plot

_____

_____

6. How could you summarize

_____

_____

7. What part of the story

_____

_____

8. When was

_____

_____

Higher-Level Thinking Questions for Language Arts
Kagan • 1 (800) 933-2667 • www.KaganOnline.com

Story
Setting

higher-level thinking questions

You can tell whether a man is clever by his answers. You can tell whether a man is wise by his questions.

— Naguib Mahfouz

Story Setting
Question Cards

Story Setting

1 What clues in the setting did the author use to tell you about the story?

Story Setting

2 How did the climate affect the action in the story?

Story Setting

3 How did the social values of the time period influence the characters?

Story Setting

4 In what other time period could the story have taken place?

Story Setting
Question Cards

Story Setting

5 In what other location could the story have taken place without affecting the plot?

Story Setting

6 How might the setting be represented by a single color?

Story Setting

7 How might the utilization of modern technology have affected the action or outcome in the story?

Story Setting

8 How might a change in transportation methods have affected the outcome?

Higher-Level Thinking Questions for Language Arts
Kagan • 1 (800) 933-2667 • www.KaganOnline.com

Story Setting
Question Cards

Story Setting

9 Which material would you choose to portray the setting; paint, clay, or water colors? Explain your choice.

Story Setting

10 How is the action of the story dependent on the setting?

Story Setting

11 How might a travel agent describe the setting?

Story Setting

12 Where did the story take place?

Story Setting
Question Cards

Story Setting

13 When did the story take place?

Story Setting

14 Name the continent on which the story takes place. What changes would have occurred in the story if it had been set on a different continent?

Story Setting

15 If the setting of the story were pictured in a magazine, what might the caption below the picture say?

Story Setting

16 Would you like to live in the time period in which the story takes place? Why or why not?

Story Setting
Journal Writing Question

Write your response to the question below.
Be ready to share your response.

How is the action of the story dependent on the setting?

_____

_____

_____

_____

_____

_____

_____

_____

_____

_____

_____

_____

_____

_____

_____

_____

_____

_____

_____

Story Setting

Question Starters

Use the question starters below to create complete questions.
Send your questions to a partner or to another team to answer.

1. What role did the setting

2. If the story was set

3. How did the characters

4. What features of the setting

5. How could you describe

6. Would you prefer

7. Where else

8. When might

138

Story Structure

higher-level thinking questions

The word question is derived from the Latin quaerere (to seek) which is the same root as the word for quest. A creative life is a continued quest, and good questions can be very useful guides. Most useful are open-ended questions; they allow for fresh unanticipated answers to reveal themselves.

— Source Unknown

Story Structure
Question Cards

Story Structure

1 What was the main conflict in the story?

Story Structure

2 Was there a moment the author made us feel the most suspense? When?

Story Structure

3 Create a new ending to the story you would like better.

Story Structure

4 Were you surprised by the ending? Why, or why not?

Story Structure

5 How did the author make us feel the conflict was important?

Story Structure

6 Some conflicts are inside one person, like when you want something and wish you did not. What kind of conflicts did the character have?

Story Structure

7 What caused the story to end the way it did: The character's luck, hard work, skill, or a bright idea? Which is more important in real life?

Story Structure

8 What hints did the author give us about how the story would end?

Story Structure
Question Cards

Story Structure

9 If you were to rewrite the story for a different time period, when would it be? Why? How would it change the story?

Story Structure

10 Try to improve the story by adding or subtracting a character. Who would it be? How would this improve the story?

Story Structure

11 At what point did you like the main character most? Least?

Story Structure

12 Give a character in the story a new name which better fits his/her personality? Explain why.

Story Structure
Question Cards

13 If you were to place the story in a different place, where would it be? Why? How would this change the story?

14 How much time passed from the beginning to the end of the story? Would the story be better if it took more or less time? Why?

15 Dress the main character differently. Why did you choose the outfit you did?

16 If the main character found someone hurt in the street, would she or he help? What makes you think so?

Higher-Level Thinking Questions for Language Arts
Kagan • 1 (800) 933-2667 • www.KaganOnline.com

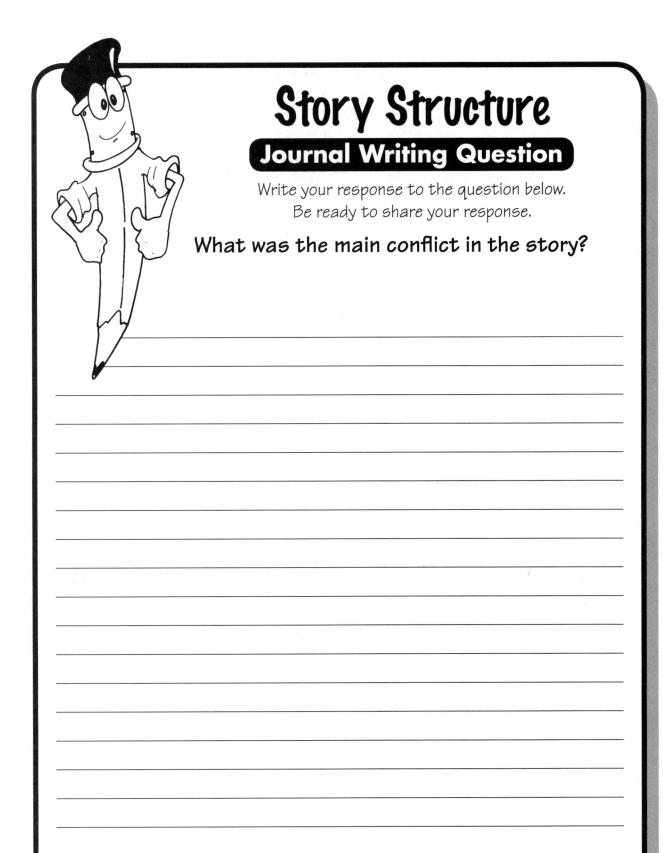

Story Structure

Journal Writing Question

Write your response to the question below.
Be ready to share your response.

What was the main conflict in the story?

Story Structure
Question Starters

Use the question starters below to create complete questions.
Send your questions to a partner or to another team to answer.

1. Did the setting

2. How were the characters

3. If you changed the plot

4. What point of view

5. How could you improve

6. What sequence of events

7. Why was the conflict

8. Did the climax

Higher-Level Thinking Questions for Language Arts
Kagan • 1 (800) 933-2667 • www.KaganOnline.com

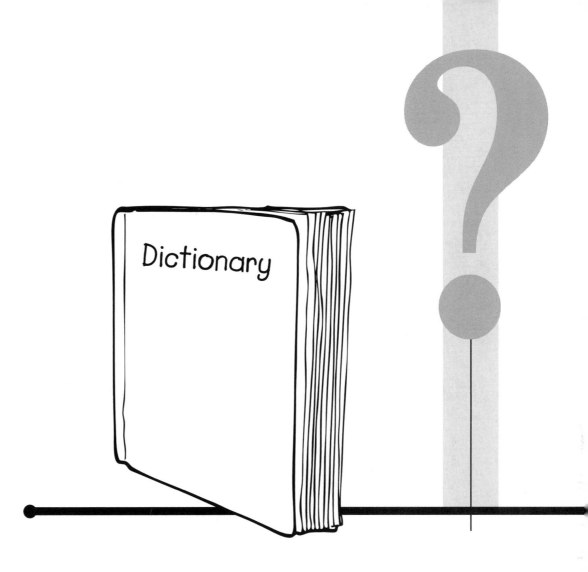

Vocabulary

higher-level thinking questions

"There are lots of people who cannot think seriously without injuring their minds.

— John Jay Chapman"

Vocabulary
Question Cards

Vocabulary

1 If the vocabulary word was part of an answer, what would be the question?

Vocabulary

2 Share a possible crossword puzzle clue for the vocabulary word.

Vocabulary

3 Name two antonyms for the vocabulary word.

Vocabulary

4 Compare and contrast the different definitions of the vocabulary word.

Vocabulary
Question Cards

Vocabulary

5 How could you represent the word's meaning with a symbol(s)?

Vocabulary

6 Use the vocabulary word in a figure of speech (metaphor or simile).

Vocabulary

7 What other words can you create from the letters of the vocabulary word?

Vocabulary

8 Use the vocabulary word in a sentence with alliteration.

Higher-Level Thinking Questions for Language Arts
Kagan • 1 (800) 933-2667 • www.KaganOnline.com

Vocabulary
Question Cards

Vocabulary
9 Paraphrase the dictionary definition of the vocabulary word.

Vocabulary
10 Add a prefix or suffix to the vocabulary word and tell the meaning of the new word.

Vocabulary
11 What are the dictionary guide words for the vocabulary word?

Vocabulary
12 Name two words that rhyme with the vocabulary word.

Vocabulary

13 Use the vocabulary word in an exclamatory sentence.

Vocabulary

14 Name two synonyms for the word.

Vocabulary

15 What is the pronunciation and number of syllables given in the dictionary.

Vocabulary

16 What part of speech is the vocabulary word? How might it be used as another part of speech?

Higher-Level Thinking Questions for Language Arts
Kagan • 1 (800) 933-2667 • www.KaganOnline.com

Vocabulary

Journal Writing Question

Write your response to the question below.
Be ready to share your response.

Use the vocabulary word in a figure of speech (metaphor or simile).

Vocabulary
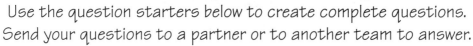
Question Starters

Use the question starters below to create complete questions.
Send your questions to a partner or to another team to answer.

1. How would you define _____

_____

2. How could this word _____

_____

3. What is another word _____

_____

4. What does this word _____

_____

5. How could you use _____

_____

6. When have you heard _____

_____

7. What is another way to say _____

_____

8. Does this word _____

_____

Higher-Level Thinking Questions for Language Arts
Kagan • 1 (800) 933-2667 • www.KaganOnline.com